3   tablespoons granulated sugar
½   teaspoon baking powder

Preheat the oven to 400° F.

In a large bowl combine the brown sugar, cornstarch, lemon juice, nutmeg, cloves, the dash of salt, and 1 teaspoon of the cinnamon. Add the apples and toss them until they are well coated. Spread the apple mixture evenly in the pie shell.

In a glass bowl combine the melted butter with the flour, sugar, baking powder, the remaining ½ teaspoon cinnamon, and the remaining ⅛ teaspoon salt. Spread the streusel evenly over the pie filling.

Bake the pie for 40 to 45 minutes, or until the apples are tender and the streusel topping is lightly browned. Cool the pie on a rack before serving. Serves 8.

## Lemon Chess Pie

¼   cup (½ stick) butter
1½  cups sugar
4   eggs
    juice of 2–3 lemons
1   scant tablespoon cornmeal
1   unbaked pastry shell

Preheat oven to 350°F.

In a mixing bowl cream together the butter and sugar until light. Add the eggs and stir until blended. Add the lemon juice and cornmeal. Pour the mixture into the pie shell and bake the pie for about 25 minutes. Serve warm or cold. Makes 1 pie.

## Plum Tart

2   cups flour
½   teaspoon salt
½   teaspoon baking powder
2   teaspoons sugar
1   cup (2 sticks) butter, softened and cut
    into pieces
5   egg yolks
⅓   cup cold water
¼   cup bread crumbs
2   pounds fresh plums, halved and pitted
1   cup plus 2 tablespoons sugar
2   egg yolks
2   tablespoons cream

Preheat the oven to 325° F.

Sift together the flour, salt, baking powder, and sugar. Cut in two thirds of the butter and blend the mixture well. Make a well in the center and add 3 of the egg yolks and the water. Stir the mixture until it becomes a dough. Knead the dough thoroughly, cover it with plastic wrap, and refrigerate it for 1 hour.

Turn the dough out onto a lightly floured surface and roll it into a thin circle. Crimp the edges to form a 1-inch collar. Transfer the shell to a baking sheet, sprinkle it with bread crumbs, and dot it with the remaining butter.

Arrange the plum halves in rows, cut side down, in the shell. Sprinkle them with 1 cup of the sugar. In a bowl beat the 2 egg yolks until they are smooth. Stir in the remaining 2 tablespoons sugar and the cream and pour the mixture over the plums. Bake the tart for 45 minutes. Makes 6 servings.

# Cherry Tart

2 *1-pound cans pitted sour red cherries*
  *packed in water*
2 *tablespoons kirsch*
1 *cup sugar*
2 *cups flour*
⅛ *teaspoon salt*
⅔ *cup butter*
1 *egg, lightly beaten*
1 *tablespoon water*
2 *teaspoons grated lemon rind*
4 *teaspoons cornstarch*
¼ *teaspoon almond extract*
½ *cup heavy cream, whipped*

Drain the cherries, reserving the liquid, and sprinkle them with the kirsch and ⅔ cup of the sugar. Let them stand at room temperature for 1 hour, stirring occasionally.

Into a large bowl sift together the flour, the salt, and the remaining ⅓ cup sugar. Cut in the butter until the mixture resembles fine meal. Make a well in the center of the dry ingredients and add the egg, water, and lemon rind. Combine the mixture until the dough sticks together and forms a ball. Turn the dough out onto a lightly floured board and knead it three or four times. Reshape the dough into a ball, wrap it in wax paper or plastic, and chill it for 30 minutes.

Pat the dough into a 9-inch tart or pie pan, pressing it out evenly over the bottom and up the sides of the pan. Crimp the edges of the pastry, prick the bottom with a fork, and refrigerate the shell for 10 minutes.

Preheat the oven to 350° F.

Drain the cherries well, pour the kirsch marinade into a measuring cup, and add enough of the reserved liquid from the cherries to make one cup. In a saucepan combine the kirsch mixture with the cornstarch. Bring the liquid to a boil, stirring, and simmer it for 2 to 3 minutes, or until it is clear and thickened. Pour it over the drained cherries, add the almond extract, and stir the mixture gently. Pour the cherry mixture into the chilled tart shell and bake the tart for 50 minutes, or until crust is golden and the filling is bubbly. Serve the tart, warm or cold, with the whipped cream. Makes 8 servings.

# Sour Cream Apple Tart

  *pastry for a 1-crust 9-inch tart*
1 *pound tart cooking apples*
2 *tablespoons lemon juice*
1 *cup sour cream*
½ *cup granulated sugar*
2 *eggs*
2 *tablespoons flour*
½ *teaspoon cinnamon*
½ *teaspoon grated lemon rind*
¼ *cup firmly packed dark brown sugar*

Preheat the oven to 375° F.

Line the bottom of a 9-inch shallow tart pan with pastry dough, crimp the edges of the pastry, and prick the bottom of the shell with a fork. Bake the shell for 15 minutes, or until it is slightly browned. Let the tart shell cool on a rack.

Peel and core the apples, thinly slice them into a bowl, and toss with the lemon juice. Arrange the apple slices in the tart shell in concentric circles. In a bowl combine the sour cream, granulated sugar, eggs, flour, cinnamon, and lemon rind, stirring to blend the mixture well. Pour the filling over the apples and sprinkle it with the brown sugar. Bake the tart for 40 to 45 minutes, until the filling is set, rotating it once during the baking time. Let the tart cool on a rack and chill it thoroughly before serving. Makes 8 servings.

## Vanilla Bavarian Cream with Raspberry Sauce

### BAVARIAN CREAM

| | |
|---|---|
| 1 | tablespoon (1 envelope) unflavored gelatin |
| 1/2 | cup sugar |
| 1/8 | teaspoon salt |
| 2 | egg yolks |
| 1 1/4 | cups milk |
| 1 | teaspoon vanilla |
| 2 | egg whites |
| 1 | cup heavy cream, whipped |

### RASPBERRY SAUCE

| | |
|---|---|
| 1 | 10-ounce package frozen raspberries, thawed and their liquid reserved |
| 1/4 | cup sugar |
| 1/4 | cup Port wine |
| 1 | tablespoon cornstarch |
| 1 | tablespoon lemon juice |
| 1/8 | teaspoon salt |
| 2 | tablespoons butter |

To make the Bavarian cream, in the top of a double boiler combine the gelatin, 1/4 cup of the sugar, and the salt. In a small bowl beat the egg yolks with the milk; stir the mixture into the dry ingredients in the double boiler. Cook the custard over hot water, stirring constantly, until the gelatin is dissolved, about 6 minutes. Remove the custard from the heat and stir in the vanilla. Refrigerate the mixture until it mounds slightly when dropped from a spoon.

In a large bowl beat the egg whites until they are stiff but not dry. Gradually beat in the remaining 1/4 cup sugar and continue to beat the meringue until it is very stiff. Fold the gelatin mixture into the beaten egg whites. Gently fold in the whipped cream and turn the mixture into an oiled 5-cup mold. Refrigerate the Bavarian cream for at least 2 hours, or until it is set.

To make the raspberry sauce, in a saucepan combine the raspberries and their liquid with the 1/4 cup sugar and the Port. In a measuring cup combine the cornstarch with the lemon juice. Pour the paste into the raspberries and cook the sauce over low heat, stirring often, until the sauce is thickened and clear. Remove the sauce from the heat, add the 1/8 teaspoon salt and the butter, and stir the sauce until the butter is melted. Strain the sauce and chill it until serving time, or serve it warm, without straining.

Rap the gelatin mold sharply against a hard surface, submerge the bottom of the mold in warm water for a few seconds, and invert the mold on a serving plate. Serve the raspberry sauce as an accompaniment. Makes 8 servings.

## Rum Puff Pudding

3   *eggs*
3/4   *cup sugar*
1/4   *teaspoon salt*
3/4   *cup half-and-half*
2/3   *cup flour*
1/2   *cup butter*
1/4   *cup dark rum*

Preheat the oven to 350° F.

In a large bowl with an electric mixer on high speed, beat together the eggs, sugar, and salt for about 6 minutes. Reduce the mixer speed to low and beat in the half-and-half and the flour just until they are blended. With a wooden spoon fold in the butter and rum. Pour the pudding into a 1½-quart soufflé dish or casserole.

Bake the pudding for 45 to 50 minutes, until it is lightly browned and set. Serve it warm. Makes 6 servings.

## Strawberry Bavarian Cream

2   *eggs*
2   *tablespoons sugar*
1½   *cups milk, scalded*
3   *envelopes unflavored gelatin*
1/2   *cup water*
4   *cups strained strawberry purée (about 3 pints berries)*
3/4   *cup sugar*
1   *cup heavy cream, whipped*

In a large bowl beat the eggs with the sugar until the mixture is smooth. Gradually stir in the hot milk. Pour the mixture into a saucepan and heat it over low heat, stirring constantly until the custard coats the spoon. Strain the custard through a sieve and refrigerate it until it is cool.

In a small saucepan dissolve the gelatin in the water. Heat the mixture over low heat, stirring constantly, until the gelatin is melted. In a large bowl combine the strawberry purée and the sugar and stir the mixture until the sugar is dissolved. Stir in the gelatin mixture and chill the pudding until it begins to set. Fold in the chilled custard and the whipped cream. Turn the Bavarian cream into a serving bowl and chill it until it is set. Makes 12 servings.

## Frozen Raspberry Mousse

1   *envelope gelatin*
1/4   *cup cold water*
2   *egg yolks*
1¼   *cups milk*
1/2   *cup sugar*
    *pinch of salt*
    *vanilla*
1½   *cups raspberry purée*
2   *egg whites*
1   *cup heavy cream*
    *whipped cream to garnish*

Sprinkle the gelatin over the water and let it soften for 5 minutes. Beat the egg yolks slightly. In a heavy bottomed saucepan heat the milk until hot but not boiling. Stir about ½ cup

of the hot milk into the egg yolks, then return this mixture to the saucepan. Add the sugar, salt, and gelatin, stirring constantly over medium heat until it is slighlty thickened. Take care not to boil the mixture or the yolks will curdle. Remove the pan from the heat and chill the mixture until cool, about 20 minutes. When cool, add vanilla and raspberry purée.

Beat the egg whites until stiff and fold them into the custard. Beat the cream until it holds stiff peaks and fold it into the custard. Spoon the mixture into a 2-quart mold, cover it, and freeze it until firm. Unmold before serving and garnish with whipped cream.

## German Rice Pudding

2   cups water
½   teaspoon salt
½   cup raw long-grain rice
3   cups milk
1   tablespoon butter
½   cup sugar
½   cup raisins (optional)
1   teaspoon vanilla
    cinnamon (optional)

In a large saucepan, bring the water and salt to a boil. Add the rice and return the water to a boil. Reduce the heat and continue cooking the mixture until the water is absorbed and the rice is tender.

In another saucepan, cook the milk and the butter over low heat until the butter is melted and the milk is scalded. Pour the hot milk into the cooked rice. Bring the mixture just to a boil, lower the heat, and simmer it for 15 to 20 minutes, stirring occasionally. Sprinkle the mixture with the sugar and add the raisins, if desired. Cook the pudding over medium heat for 15 to 20 minutes more, or until it is creamy. Stir in the vanilla.

Serve the pudding warm, sprinkled with cinnamon, if desired. Makes 6 servings.

## Red Fruit Pudding

1    1-pound can pitted tart red cherries in
     heavy syrup
1    10-ounce package frozen raspberries,
     thawed, juice reserved
1½   tablespoons cornstarch
1    tablespoon lemon juice
1    tablespoon currant jelly
1    cup sweetened whipped cream

Drain the cherries and raspberries, reserving and combining the liquids. Purée the fruits in a blender or in a food processor fitted with the steel blade. Force the puréed fruits through a fine sieve to remove the raspberry seeds. In a saucepan, stir together the cornstarch and about ½ cup of the reserved raspberry-cherry juice. Add the remaining juice and bring the mixture to a boil, stirring, until it is thickened and bubbly. Stir in the lemon juice and currant jelly. Fold in the fruit, let the pudding cool, and refrigerate it until it is cold. Serve the pudding in a glass bowl or in individual sherbet dishes and top each serving with whipped cream. Makes 5–6 servings.

## Lemon Sherbet

2   *cups sugar*
3   *cups water*
1   *lemon, very thinly sliced*
    *juice of 6 lemons*
4   *egg whites*

In a saucepan combine the sugar, 2 cups of the water, and the lemon slices. Bring the mixture to a boil and cook it, stirring, for 5 minutes. Strain the syrup into a bowl. Combine the lemon juice with the remaining 1 cup water and stir the mixture into the syrup. Freeze the mixture in an electric ice cream freezer according to the manufacturer's instructions until it is half frozen.

With an electric mixer beat the egg whites until they hold stiff peaks. Fold the meringue into the half-frozen sherbet. Spoon the sherbet into freezer trays and freeze it completely. Makes 10 servings.

## Fresh Peach Sherbet

1½   *cups sugar*
½   *cup water*
3   *cups sliced fresh peaches*
    *juice of 2 oranges*
1   *teaspoon fresh lemon juice*
2   *egg whites, stiffly beaten*
1   *cup heavy cream, whipped*

In a saucepan combine the sugar and water and cook the mixture until it forms a thread when dropped from a wooden spoon. Remove

the pan from the heat and let the mixture cool. In a bowl mash the peaches coarsely with a fork or the back of a wooden spoon, but do not purée them. Stir the cooked syrup into the mashed peaches. Add the orange juice and the lemon juice and blend the mixture well. Turn the mixture into freezer trays and freeze it until it is almost firm. Transfer the sherbet to a large bowl, beat it well, and fold in the beaten egg whites and then the whipped cream. Return the sherbet to the freezer and let it harden, stirring several times during the freezing process. Makes 8 servings.

## Strawberry Ice Cream

2   *pints strawberries, hulled*
1   *cup granulated sugar*
½   *cup* **framboise** *(raspberry liqueur)*
1   *large egg*
1   *cup half-and-half*
3   *cups heavy cream*

In a saucepan combine half of the strawberries with ½ cup of the sugar and heat the mixture over low heat for 10 minutes. Purée the mixture in a blender and let it cool. Put the remaining strawberries in a bowl, pour the *framboise* over them, and let them marinate for 10 minutes. In another bowl with an electric mixer, combine the egg, the half-and-half, and the remaining ½ cup sugar and beat the mixture until it is smooth and the sugar is dissolved. Gradually add the heavy cream and beat the mixture for 1 minute more. Transfer the mixture to an ice cream maker and freeze

it according to the manufacturer's directions. When the mixture is half frozen, add the strawberry purée. Fold marinated strawberries into the frozen ice cream end. Makes 6 servings.

## Fresh Apricot Ice Cream

2  *pounds apricots, peeled, pitted, and halved*
1¼  *cups sugar*
⅛  *teaspoon salt*
1  *tablespoon vanilla*
2  *cups heavy cream*
2  *cups light cream*
1  *cup milk*

Purée the apricots in a blender or in a food processor fitted with the steel blade. In a large bowl combine the purée with the sugar, salt, vanilla, the heavy and light cream, and the milk, stirring to blend the mixture well. Freeze the mixture in a 4-quart ice cream maker. Makes 8–12 servings.

## Apple Dumplings

1  *cup granulated sugar*
1  *teaspoon cinnamon*
⅛  *teaspoon ground cloves*
¼  *teaspoon salt*
¾  *cup plus 1 tablespoon water*
   *Pastry for 2-crust 9-inch pie*
6  *medium-size tart apples*
1  *egg white*
6  *tablespoons brown sugar*
6  *tablespoons raisins*
3  *tablespoons butter*
1  *cup heavy cream, whipped (optional)*

In a 9- x 13-inch flameproof baking pan combine the granulated sugar, cinnamon, cloves, salt, and the ¾ cup water. Cover the pan and cook the mixture on top of the stove, stirring, until it is syrupy. Remove the pan from the heat and set it aside.

Preheat the oven to 425° F.

Cut the pastry into 6 equal pieces. On a lightly floured surface roll each piece into a round large enough to enclose one apple. Peel and core the apples. In a small bowl beat the egg white with the remaining 1 tablespoon water and brush the mixture around the edge of each round of dough. Place one apple on each pastry circle. Spoon 1 tablespoon brown sugar and 1 tablespoon raisins into each apple. Gather the pastry up around each apple, leaving it open at the top, like a sack. Brush the remaining egg white around the inside of the pastry-sack opening and press the dough together, closing the package. Set the dough-wrapped apples in the syrup in the baking dish. Top each apple dumpling with ½ tablespoon butter.

Bake the dough-wrapped apples for 10 minutes. Reduce the oven temperature to 350° F. and bake them for 40 minutes more, or until they are tender and the pastry is browned. Let the apples cool until they are just warm and serve them topped with the syrup and the whipped cream, if desired. Makes 6 servings.

# Apples Baked in Apricot Sauce

**BAKED APPLES**

|   |   |
|---|---|
| 6 | *tart baking apples* |
| 1/2 | *cup honey, heated* |
| 1/3 | *cup sliced blanched almonds* |
| 2 | *1-pound cans pitted apricots in syrup* |

**VANILLA APRICOT SAUCE**

|   |   |
|---|---|
| 1 | *cup heavy cream* |
| 1 | *pint vanilla ice cream, softened* |
| 2 | *tablespoons apricot brandy* |

To make the baked apples, core the apples and peel them, leaving a 1-inch strip of skin around the bottom. Arrange them in a well-buttered shallow casserole or gratin dish just large enough to hold them. Fill the cavity of each apple with 1 tablespoon honey and brush the remaining honey over the apples. Sprinkle the apples with the slivered almonds.

Preheat the oven to 400° F.

Drain the apricots, reserving 1/2 cup of the syrup. Purée the apricots with the reserved syrup in a food processor or blender. Pour the apricot purée around the apples and bake the apples for 45 minutes, basting them every 10 minutes. Let the apples cool in the casserole 30 minutes and transfer them to a serving dish.

To make the Vanilla Apricot Sauce, in a chilled bowl beat the heavy cream until it stands up in soft peaks. In another bowl beat together the ice cream and the apricot brandy until the mixture is smooth. Fold the whipped cream into the ice cream and chill the sauce for at least 1 hour.

Serve the baked apples, warm, with the sauce. Makes 6 servings.

# Apple Crisp with Eggnog Sauce

**EGGNOG SAUCE**

|   |   |
|---|---|
| 12 | *egg yolks* |
| 3/4 | *cup granulated sugar* |
| 4 | *cups half-and-half, scalded* |
| 3 | *tablespoons rum* |
| 1 | *teaspoon vanilla* |
| 1/4 | *teaspoon nutmeg* |

**APPLE CRISP**

|   |   |
|---|---|
| 9 | *large Granny Smith apples* |
| 9 | *large Golden Delicious apples* |
| 1 1/2 | *cups (3 sticks) unsalted butter, cut into pieces* |
| 1/2 | *cup granulated sugar* |
| 1/4 | *teaspoon cinnamon* |
| 1 | *teaspooon vanilla* |
| 2 | *cups flour* |
| 2 | *cups dark brown sugar* |

To make the eggnog sauce, in a bowl whisk together the egg yolks and granulated sugar until they are well blended. Gradually whisk in the half-and-half. Pour the mixture into the top of a double boiler and cook it over simmering water, stirring constantly, for 10 to 15 minutes, until it is thick enough to coat the back of a metal spoon or until a thermometer registers 180° F. Strain the sauce through a fine sieve into a medium bowl. Place the bowl in a larger bowl half filled with ice water. Stir in the rum, vanilla, and nutmeg and let the sauce cool to room temperature, stirring occasionally. Refrigerate the sauce, covered, for 3 to 4 hours.

To make the apple crisp, peel and core the apples and cut them into 3/4-inch chunks. In a

large heavy saucepan melt ½ cup (1 stick) of the butter over high heat. Add the apples and sauté them, stirring constantly, for 5 minutes. Reduce the heat to medium and stir in the sugar. Cook the apples, stirring frequently and mashing them slightly with a wooden spoon, for 30 to 35 minutes, until all of the liquid is evaporated and the apples form a chunky sauce. Remove the apples from the heat, stir in the cinnamon and vanilla, and add more sugar, if desired. Set the apples aside to cool slightly.

Heat the oven to 375° F. and butter a 15- x 9½- x 2-inch baking pan.

In a bowl combine the flour and brown sugar. Cut in the remaining 1 cup (2 sticks) butter until the mixture is crumbly. Spread the applesauce evenly in the pan and top it with a layer of the flour mixture. Bake the crisp for 45 to 60 minutes, until the topping is set and golden and the applesauce is bubbling. Let the crisp cool to lukewarm on a rack and serve it with the sauce. Makes 12–16 servings.

# Pink Applesauce

¾  *cup water*
½  *cup sugar*
¼  *cup red currant jelly*
2  *tablespoons lemon juice*
6  *tart apples*

In a heavy saucepan combine the water, sugar, jelly, and lemon juice. Cook the mixture over high heat, stirring constantly, until the sugar is dissolved. Bring the syrup to a boil, reduce the heat, and simmer it for 5 minutes.

Peel, core, and thinly slice the apples. Stir them into the syrup and simmer them for 10 to 15 minutes, until they are soft. With a slotted spoon transfer the apple slices to a blender or food processor and purée them. Cook the syrup over high heat until it is reduced and thickened. In a bowl combine the puréed apples with the syrup. Refrigerate the sauce and serve it with gingerbread. Makes 6 servings.

# Glazed Baked Apples

1  *cup sugar*
½  *teaspoon cinnamon*
1½  *cups water*
1  *tablespoon fresh lemon juice*
2  *tablespoons fresh orange juice*
6  *baking apples*

Preheat the oven to 350° F.

In a saucepan combine 1 cup of the sugar with the cinnamon, water, lemon juice, and orange juice. Bring the mixture to a boil and cook it at a fast simmer for 5 minutes, stirring occasionally until the sugar is dissolved and the mixture becomes a syrup. Remove the syrup from the heat.

Remove three-fourths of the core from each apple and peel a 1½-inch strip from around the stem end. Arrange the apples in a baking pan or dish, pour the syrup into and over them, and bake the apples for 1 hour, or until they are tender, basting occasionally with the syrup. Makes 6 servings.

## Peach Cobbler

**FILLING**

|       |                              |
|-------|------------------------------|
| 5     | tablespoons cornstarch       |
| 2–2½  | cups sugar                   |
| 8     | cups sliced fresh peaches    |
| ½     | teaspoon almond extract      |
| ¼     | cup (½ stick) butter, melted |

**PASTRY**

|     |                          |
|-----|--------------------------|
| ½   | cup shortening           |
| 2   | cups flour               |
| 4   | tablespoons sugar        |
|     | Pinch salt               |
| 4–5 | tablespoons ice water    |
| 3   | tablespoons butter, melted |

To make the filling, blend the cornstarch and 2 cups of the sugar and toss in the peaches, almond extract, and melted butter. Taste the mixture and add the remaining sugar, if desired.

Preheat the oven to 400° F. and butter a 9-×-13-inch baking pan.

To make the pastry, cut the shortening into the flour until the mixture is mealy. Add 2 tablespoons of the sugar and the pinch of salt. Gradually add enough of the ice water to make a dough that will hold its shape. Roll the dough out on a floured surface and cut it into five 1-×-13-inch strips and seven 1-×-9-inch strips.

Pour the peach mixture into the baking pan. Crisscross the dough strips over the filling, brush the dough with the melted butter, and sprinkle it with the remaining 2 tablespoons sugar. Bake the cobbler for 30 minutes, or until the crust is browned. Makes 10–12 servings.

## Zesty Fruit Compote

|       |                                      |
|-------|--------------------------------------|
| 1     | pound dried apricots                 |
| ⅔     | cup sugar                            |
| ½     | teaspoon salt                        |
|       | juice of 1 lemon                     |
|       | rind of 1 lemon in large pieces      |
|       | juice of 1 orange                    |
|       | rind of 1 orange in large pieces     |
| 2     | cups dry white wine                  |
| 1½    | cups pitted and halved prunes        |
| 1     | cup diced pineapple with its juice   |
| 1     | can drained white peaches            |
| ½     | cup slivered almonds                 |
| 2     | tablespoons grated candied ginger    |
| ½     | cup rum or Grand Marnier             |
| 1–2   | cups seedless white grapes           |
| 1–2   | cups sliced strawberries, if desired |

In a saucepan combine the apricots, sugar, salt, lemon juice and rind, orange juice and rind, and white wine. Bring the mixture to a boil, reduce the heat, and simmer it until the apricots are tender, about 20 minutes. Stir in the prunes and cook the mixture for 5 minutes more, or until the prunes are tender. Remove the lemon and orange rind and stir in the pineapple with its juice, the peaches, and the almonds. Add the ginger, rum, grapes, and, if desired, the strawberries. Heat the mixture through and serve it warm with whipped cream as a dessert or chilled with roast meat or poultry. Makes 8–10 servings.

## Apricot Poached Pears

6  *medium-size pears (about 2 pounds)*
1  *tablespoon lemon juice*
1  *cup water*
1  *cup white wine*
½  *cup sugar*
⅓  *cup chopped dried apricots*
1  *teaspoon grated orange rind*
1  *cinnamon stick*
2  *tablespoons toasted sliced almonds*

Preheat the oven to 300° F.

Peel the pears, leaving the stems intact. Use a grapefruit knife and small spoon to hollow out the cores, working from the bottom of the fruit. In a bowl combine the lemon juice with ½ cup of the water. Dip the pears in the lemon juice mixture and set them aside to drain. In a 2- to 2½-quart casserole with a cover, combine the wine, sugar, apricots, orange rind, cinnamon stick, and the remaining ½ cup water. Arrange the pears stem end up in the sauce and bake them, covered, for 1 hour, or until they are tender, adding more water if necessary. Let the pears cool in the cooking liquid.

With a slotted spoon transfer the cool pears to a serving dish. Remove the cinnamon stick from the sauce and purée the sauce in a blender or food processor until it is smooth and thick. Spoon the sauce over the pears and sprinkle the dessert with the almonds. Makes 6 servings.

## Almond-Apple Crunch

1¼  *cups flour*
¾  *cup (1½ sticks) butter, softened*
½  *cup almond paste*
1½  *cups sugar*
¼  *cup soft fine bread crumbs*
6  *tart apples*
   *juice of 1 lemon*
   *pinch salt*
½  *teaspoon ground cinnamon*
   *pinch ground cloves*
   *pinch nutmeg*

Combine the flour, butter, almond paste, and 1 cup of the sugar in a bowl and refrigerate the mixture for 2 hours.

Preheat the oven to 350° F. Butter a 9- x 13-inch baking dish and coat it with the bread crumbs.

Peel and core the apples and slice them thinly into a large bowl. Toss the apples with the lemon juice, salt, cinnamon, cloves, nutmeg, and the remaining ½ cup sugar. Turn the apple mixture into the baking dish and crumble the almond paste mixture over it. Bake the crisp for 45 minutes, or until the top is golden brown. Makes 6−8 servings.

# RESOURCE GUIDE

Many department and specialty stores throughout the country often carry, especially at holiday times; special molds, forms and utensils for traditional baked goods and other German-American specialties. Mail-order culinary catalogues, such are those listed below, are also often good resources for such items.

Lekvar by the Barrel, 1577 First Avenue, New York, New York 10028.

Williams-Sonoma, P.O. Box 3792, San Francisco, California 94119.

The Silo, Upland Road, New Milford, Connecticut 06776.

Many state and local organizations have issued attractive and interesting regional cookbooks. The following are among the many excellent ones available.

*Big Valley Amish Cookbook: A Cookbook from Kishacoquillas Valley.* Available by mail from Mr. and Mrs. Joe A. Zook, R1, Box 207, Belleville, Pa., 17004

*Colorado Cache Cookbook*, available by mail at a cost of $12.95 per copy plus $1.30 per copy for postage and handling from The Junior League of Denver, Inc., 3372 South Broadway, Englewood, Colorado 80110.

*Guten Appetit!*, available by mail at a cost of $11.43 plus $1.25 for postage and handling (Texas residents please add $.57 per copy for local sales tax) from The Sophienburg Memorial Association, Inc., New Braunfels, Texas 78130.

*The Mennonite Maid Cookbook*, available by mail from Legacy Book Publishers, Route 2, Dayton, Virginia 22821.

*San Francisco a la Carte*, available by mail at a cost of $19.95 plus $2.50 for postage and handling (plus tax in California) from The Junior League of San Francisco, Inc., 2226 Fillmore Street, San Francisco, California 94115.

*Soupçon II*, available by mail at a cost of $11.95 plus $1.55 for postage and handling (Illinois residents please add $.72 per copy for local sales tax) from The Junior League of Chicago, Inc., 1447 Astor Street, Chicago, Illinois, 60610.

# INDEX

(page numbers in italics indicate illustrations)

# ACKNOWLEDGMENTS

We wish to thank the following individuals for their help and cooperation:

Benjamin House of Rolf's German-American Restaurant, New York City; Mrs. William S. Covington, Ms. Donna Ryan, Ms. Donna Coates, Mr. Jeff Grunewald, Mr. Dan Barba.

Our thanks to the Tourist Information Bureau of the Chamber of Commerce of Fredericksburg, Texas, for the festival photographs that accompany the Introduction.

The staff of Media Projects Incorporated would like to acknowledge the help, support and cooperation of Robert Frese, Dominique Gioia and Kathy Ferguson of Taylor Publishing Company.

Kuby's Restaurant, Dallas, for their expert preparation of the food shown in the dust jacket photograph.

For information on how you can have *Better Homes and Gardens* delivered to your door, write to: Mr. Robert Austin, P.O. Box 4536, Des Moines, IA 50336.